Progress with Oxford

Multiplication, Division and Fractions

Hello! I'm Dubble.

Contents

Sparkling rows	2	Half a robot	19
2s to 100	3	Halving the apples	20
10s to 100	4	Stars in the sky	21
Rainy rows	5	Building bricks	22
5s to 100	6	Butterfly colours	23
Fruity rows	7	Look out for quarters	24
Picture it!	8	1 out of 4	25
Boats afloat!	10	Castle quarters	26
Counting candles	11	Cupcakes between 4	27
Fishy business	12	More stars in the sky	28
Grouping in 2s	13		
Grouping in 10s	14	Fishy 4s	29
Grouping in 5s	15	Colour the kites	30
Sharing it out	16	Sporty fractions	31
Spot the half	17	Progress chart	32
1 out of 2	18		

Key

 Draw

 Write

 Count

 Match

 Circle

 Colour

 Play together

 Find the sticker

Sparkling rows

 Count in 2s to find the total number of stars.

How many stars? 6

Putting objects in rows of 2 makes it easier to count them.

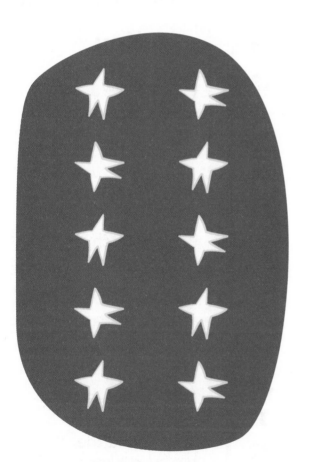

How many stars?

How many stars?

2s to 100

 Colour in every other square all the way to 100.

1	2	3	4	5	6	7	8	9	10
11	12	13	14	15	16	17	18	19	20
21	22	23	24	25	26	27	28	29	30
31	32	33	34	35	36	37	38	39	40
41	42	43	44	45	46	47	48	49	50
51	52	53	54	55	56	57	58	59	60
61	62	63	64	65	66	67	68	69	70
71	72	73	74	75	76	77	78	79	80
81	82	83	84	85	86	87	88	89	90
91	92	93	94	95	96	97	98	99	100

Do you see a **pattern**? Can you describe it?

Well done!

Give yourself a sticker

Now – track how you're doing on page 32!

10s to 100

Colour in 10s all the way to 100. 10, 20, 30, 40 ...

Can you describe this pattern?

1	2	3	4	5	6	7	8	9	10
11	12	13	14	15	16	17	18	19	20
21	22	23	24	25	26	27	28	29	30
31	32	33	34	35	36	37	38	39	40
41	42	43	44	45	46	47	48	49	50
51	52	53	54	55	56	57	58	59	60
61	62	63	64	65	66	67	68	69	70
71	72	73	74	75	76	77	78	79	80
81	82	83	84	85	86	87	88	89	90
91	92	93	94	95	96	97	98	99	100

Fill in the missing numbers.

Rainy rows

 Count in 10s to find the total number of objects.

Lining up objects in rows of 10 makes it easier to count them.

How many raindrops?

How many umbrellas?

Well done!

How many hats?

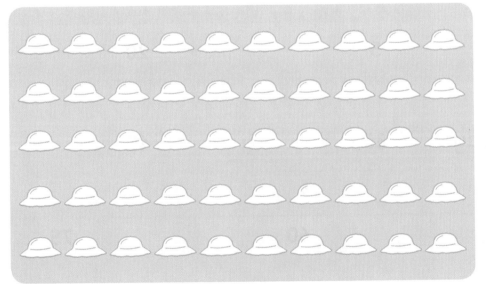

Give yourself a sticker

Now – track how you're doing on page 32!

5s to 100

 Colour in 5s all the way to 100. 5, 10, 15, 20 ...

Do you see a pattern? Can you describe it?

1	2	3	4	5	6	7	8	9	10
11	12	13	14	15	16	17	18	19	20
21	22	23	24	25	26	27	28	29	30
31	32	33	34	35	36	37	38	39	40
41	42	43	44	45	46	47	48	49	50
51	52	53	54	55	56	57	58	59	60
61	62	63	64	65	66	67	68	69	70
71	72	73	74	75	76	77	78	79	80
81	82	83	84	85	86	87	88	89	90
91	92	93	94	95	96	97	98	99	100

 Count the fingers in 5s: 5, 10, 15, 20 ... all the way to 100.

 Fill in the missing numbers.

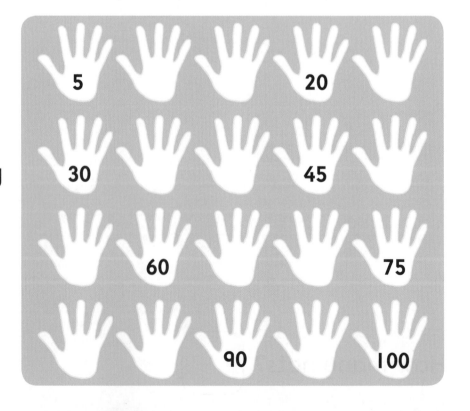

5   20

30   45

60   75

90   100

Fruity rows

 Count in 5s to find the total number of strawberries.

[ ] strawberries

Putting objects in rows of 5 makes it easier to count them.

[ ] strawberries

[ ] strawberries

[ ] strawberries

 Play with counting in blocks.

Place building blocks in 3 rows of 2 blocks. How many blocks are there altogether? How did you count them? Then place blocks in 8 rows of 2. How many blocks are there now?

Place blocks in 2 rows of 5. How many blocks are there altogether? How did you count them? Then place blocks in 5 rows of 5. How many blocks are there now?

Give yourself a sticker

Now – track how you're doing on page 32!

Picture it!

 Draw 2 apples in each bowl.

 How many apples are there altogether?

 apples

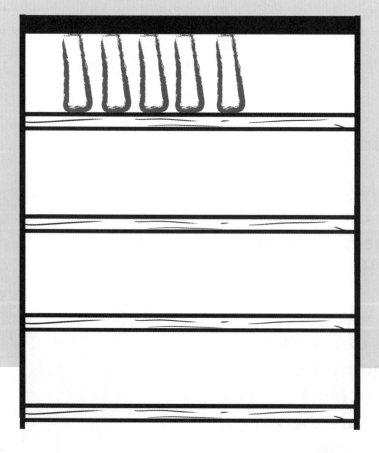

 Draw 5 books on each shelf.

How many books are there altogether?

 books

Draw 10 cupcakes on each tray.

 How many cakes are there altogether?

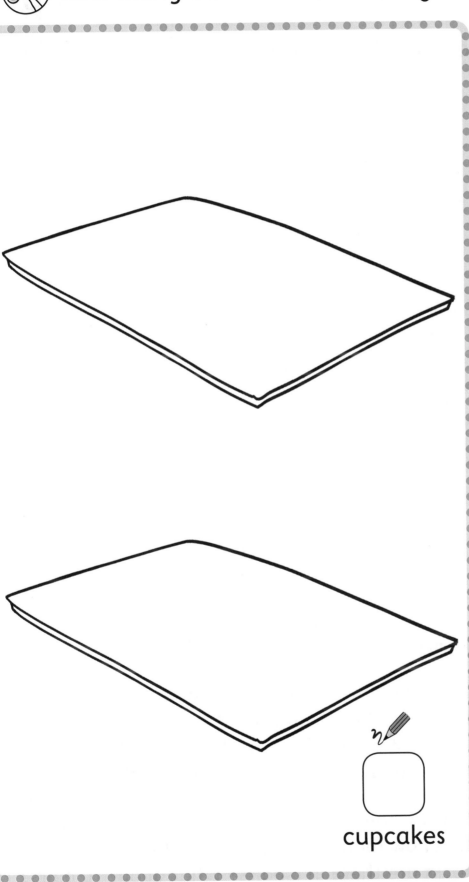

cupcakes

Well done!

Give yourself a sticker

Now – track how you're doing on page 32!

Boats afloat!

 Count in 2s to find the total number of boats.

 Match the boats to the number.

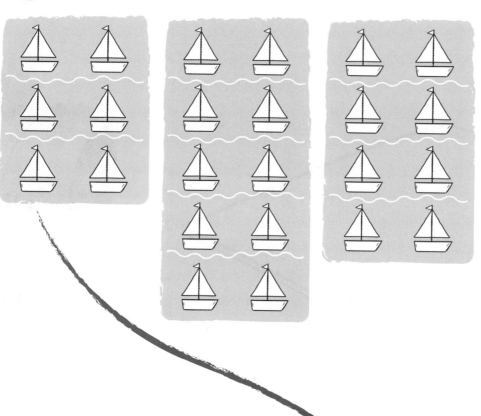

8   **12**   **6**   **10**

 Play with counting in 2s.

What can you count in 2s?

Arrange some objects in groups of 2. How quickly can you count them? Then try a different number of objects arranged in 2s. How many objects are there altogether?

Place 5 pairs of socks in a row. Count in 2s to find how many there are altogether. How many socks are there in 6 pairs? What about 10 pairs?

Counting candles

  Count in 10s to find the total number of candles.

Match the candles to the number.

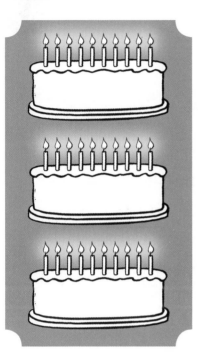

40

60

30

80

11

Fishy business

 Count in 5s to find the total number of fish.

Match the fish to the number.

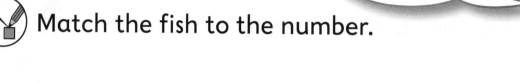
I can count in 5s: **5, 10, 15, 20, 25, 30**.

30

20

15

25

Give yourself a sticker

Now – track how you're doing on page 32!

Grouping in 2s

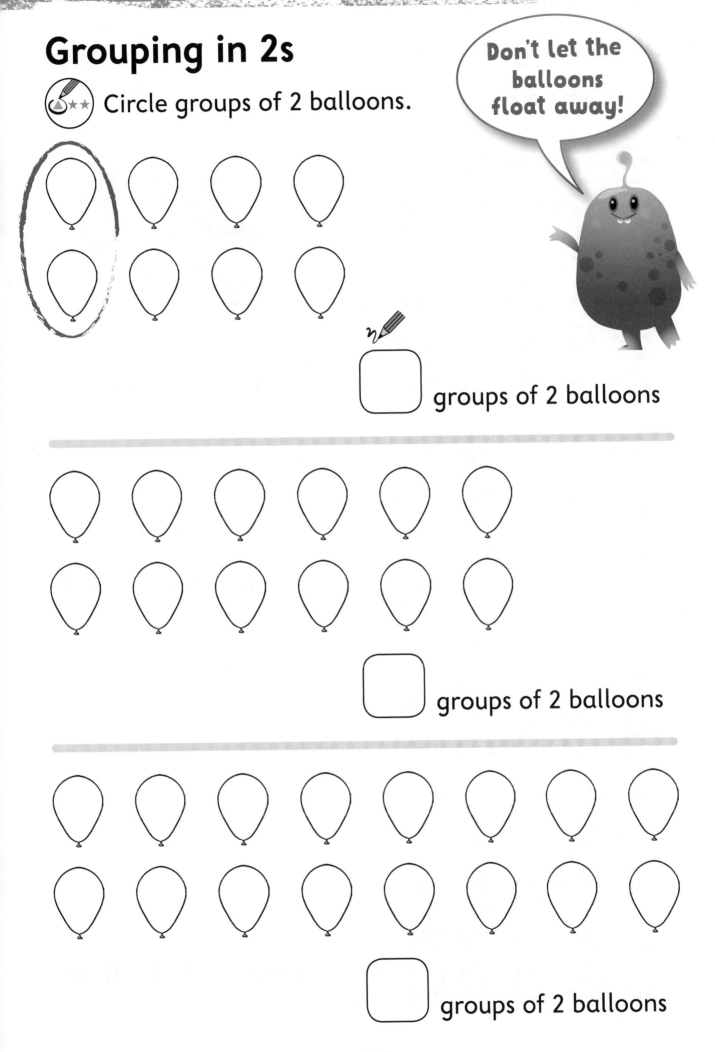

Circle groups of 2 balloons.

Don't let the balloons float away!

☐ groups of 2 balloons

☐ groups of 2 balloons

☐ groups of 2 balloons

Grouping in 10s

 ★★ Circle groups of 10 footballs.

Don't let the footballs roll away!

☐ groups of 10 footballs

☐ groups of 10 footballs

☐ groups of 10 footballs

14

Grouping in 5s

  Circle groups of 5 sheep.

Don't let the sheep run away!

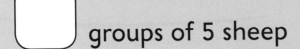

[ ] groups of 5 sheep

 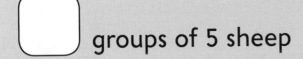

[ ] groups of 5 sheep

[ ] groups of 5 sheep

Give yourself a sticker

Now – track how you're doing on page 32!

Sharing it out

 Share 6 beads equally between 3 strings.

_____   _____

_____

 Share 15 beads equally between 5 strings.

_____   _____

_____   _____

_____

How many beads are on each string?

Give yourself a sticker

 Play with sharing.

Invite 2 teddy bears to a picnic. Share 10 biscuits between the bears equally. How many biscuits do they each get?

Build 5 equal towers from 20 construction bricks. How many bricks did you use to build each tower? Now use 30 bricks. How many bricks are in each tower?

Now – track how you're doing on page 32!

Spot the half

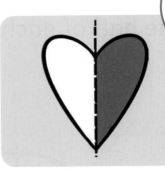

A half is 1 of 2 equal parts of something.

 Circle the shapes that have been split in half.

1 out of 2

 Colour in one half of each shape.

A half can be written as $\frac{1}{2}$.

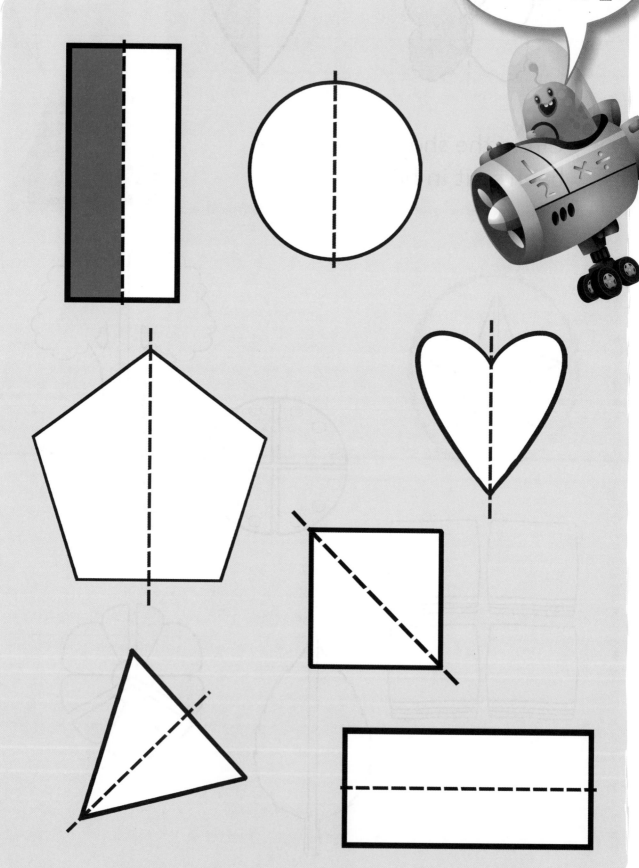

Half a robot

 Shapes have been used to build a robot.
Colour in one half of each shape.

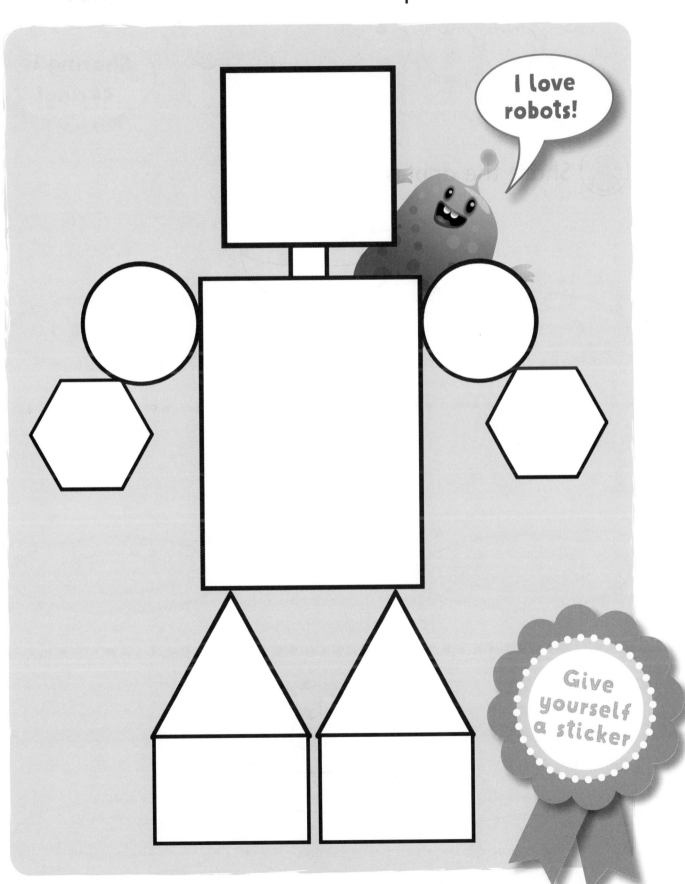

Now – track how you're doing on page 32!

Halving the apples

Sharing is caring!

Share the apples between 2.

Stars in the sky

 Draw half the number of stars.

Building bricks

 Match each set of bricks to half of that number.

I love to build!

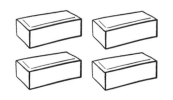

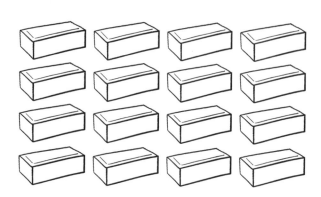

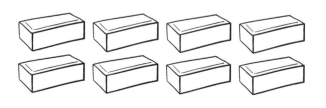

 12

16

6

18

9

4

14

2

8

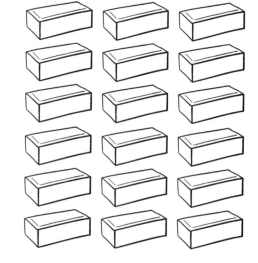

 Play with halves.

Place 6 books on a shelf. Remove half of the books. How many is one half of the books?

Bake 8 cupcakes. Offer half of the cakes to your family to eat. How many cakes were eaten? How many are left?

Give yourself a sticker

Now – track how you're doing on page 32!

Butterfly colours

 Colour half the butterflies in each group.

Flutter by, butterflies!

What number is half of 10? **5**

What number is half of 18?

What number is half of 14?

What number is half of 8?

Give yourself a sticker

Look out for quarters

A quarter is 1 of 4 equal parts of something.

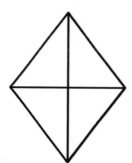
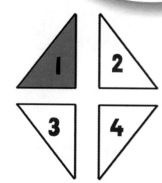

 Circle the shapes that have been split into quarters.

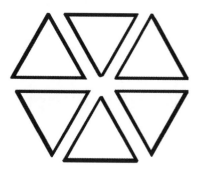

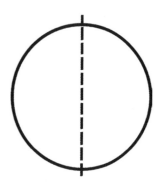
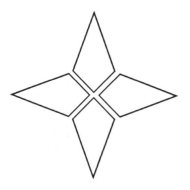

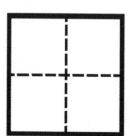

1 out of 4

 Colour in one quarter of each shape.

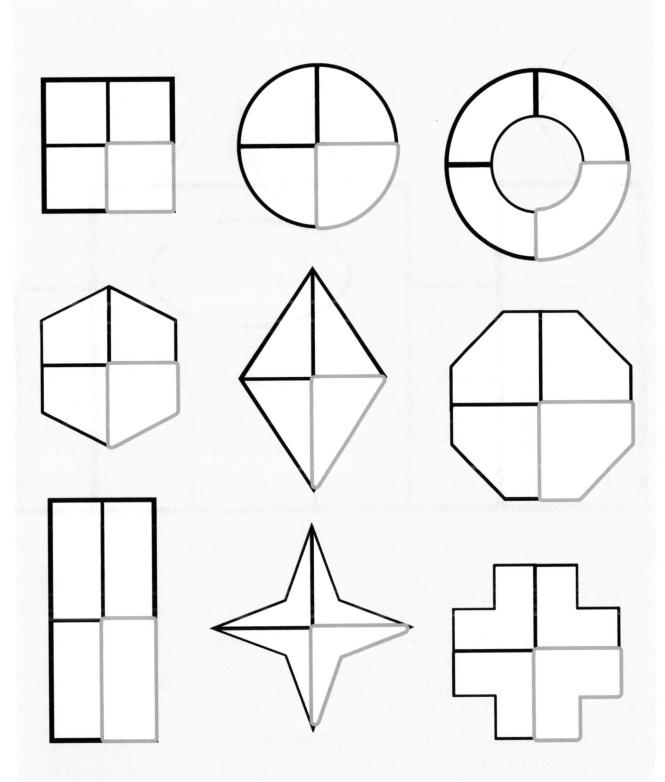

Castle quarters

 Shapes have been used to build a castle. Colour in one quarter of each shape that has not been shaded.

I'm the king of the castle!

Play with quarters.

Bake a square or circular cake. Can you cut the cake into quarters? How do you know it's been split into 4 equal parts?

Collect together pieces of paper of different sizes. How many of the papers can you fold into quarters (4 equal parts that are the same shape and size)?

Give yourself a sticker

Now – track how you're doing on page 32!

Cupcakes between 4

Think of a quarter as splitting something into 4 equal parts.

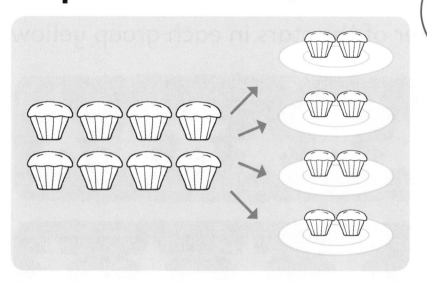

 Choose the right stickers to share the cupcakes between the 4 plates.

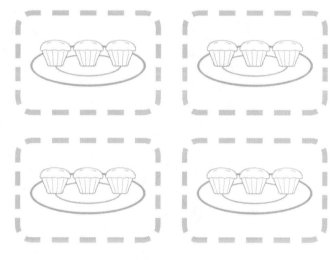

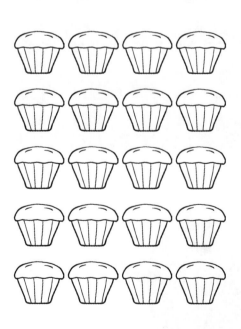

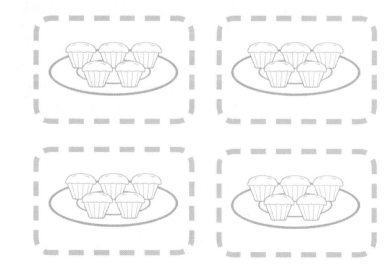

More stars in the sky

 Colour a quarter of the stars in each group yellow.

Can you find a quarter of a number?

Fishy 4s

 Match each set of fish to a quarter of that number.

Quarters in deep waters!

3

5

1

6

2

7

4

9

8

 Play with quarters.

Place 4 bananas in a fruit bowl. Remove a quarter of the bananas. How many is one quarter of 4 bananas?

Make 12 paper aeroplanes. Fly one quarter of the planes. How many of the planes were flown? How many are left?

Give yourself a sticker

Now – track how you're doing on page 32!

Colour the kites

 Colour a quarter of the kites in each group.

Have you ever flown a kite?

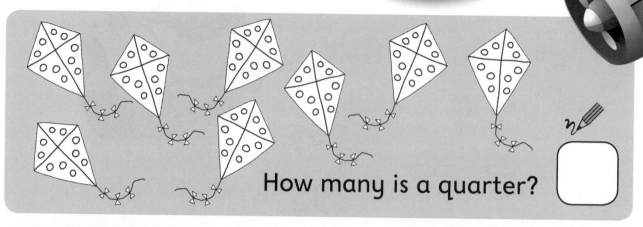

How many is a quarter?

How many is a quarter?

How many is a quarter?

How many is a quarter?

Give yourself a sticker

Now – track how you're doing on page 32!

Sporty fractions

 What fraction of each group is in pink?

Remember: $\frac{1}{2}$ means 'half' and $\frac{1}{4}$ means 'a quarter'.

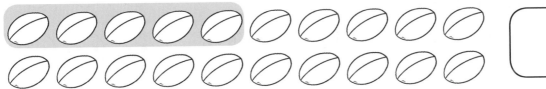

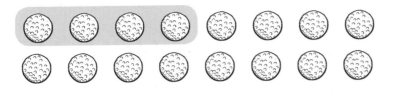

Give yourself a sticker

31

Now – track how you're doing on page 32!

Progress Chart

 Colour in a face.

☺ I can do this well

☻ I can do this but need more practice

☹ I find this difficult

Page	I Can . . .	How did you do?		
2–3	I can count a set of objects by lining them up in sets of 2 and counting in 2s.	☺	☻	☹
4–5	I can count a set of objects by lining them up in sets of 10 and counting in 10s.	☺	☻	☹
6–7	I can count a set of objects by lining them up in sets of 5 and counting in 5s.	☺	☻	☹
8–9	I can arrange objects in sets of 2, 5 or 10 and count in 2s, 5s or 10s to work out the total number of objects.	☺	☻	☹
10–12	I can count a set of objects by counting in 2s, 10s and 5s.	☺	☻	☹
13–15	I can group objects in sets of 2, 10 and 5.	☺	☻	☹
16	I can share objects between sets.	☺	☻	☹
17–19	I can spot a shape that is split into 2 equal halves and colour one half of a shape.	☺	☻	☹
20–22	I can work out the number that is half of a set of objects.	☺	☻	☹
23	I can write the number that is half of a set of objects.	☺	☻	☹
24–26	I can spot a shape that is split into 4 quarters and colour one quarter of a shape.	☺	☻	☹
27–29	I can work out the number that is a quarter of a set of objects.	☺	☻	☹
30	I can write the number that is a quarter of a set of objects.	☺	☻	☹
31	I can decide whether a set shows a quarter or a half of a set of objects.	☺	☻	☹

How did YOU do?